SELF-MYTHOLOGY

POEMS

SABA KERAMATI

THE UNIVERSITY OF ARKANSAS PRESS

FAYETTEVILLE 2024

Copyright © 2024 by Saba Keramati. All rights reserved.

ISBN: 978-1-68226-252-8
eISBN: 978-1-61075-822-2

28 27 26 25 24 5 4 3 2 1

Manufactured in the United States of America

Designed by William Clift
Cover art: *Self-Reflection*, © Hiba Schahbaz, 2015
Author photo: Marisa Kimmel

∞ The paper used in this publication meets the minimum requirements of the American National Standard for Permanence of Paper for Printed Library Materials Z39.48-1984.

Library of Congress Cataloging-in-Publication Data
Names: Keramati, Saba, author.
Title: Self-Mythology : poems / Saba Keramati.
Other titles: Self-Mythology (Compilation)
Description: Fayetteville : The University of Arkansas Press, 2024. | Series: Miller Williams
    poetry series | Summary: "Self-Mythology explores multiraciality and the legacy of exile
    alongside the poet's uniquely American origin as the only child of political refugees from
    China and Iran. Keramati navigates her ancestral past while asking what language and
    poetry can offer to those who exist on the margins of contemporary society" — Provided
    by publisher.
Identifiers: LCCN 2023053695 (print) | LCCN 2023053696 (ebook)
    ISBN 9781682262528 (paperback) | ISBN 9781610758222 (ebook)
Subjects: LCGFT: Poetry.
Classification: LCC PS3611.E726 S45 2024 (print) | LCC PS3611.E726 (ebook) |
    DDC 811/.6—dc23/eng/20231124
LC record available at https://lccn.loc.gov/2023053695
LC ebook record available at https://lccn.loc.gov/2023053696

Supported by the Miller and Lucinda Williams Poetry Fund

SELF-MYTHOLOGY

Miller Williams Poetry Series
EDITED BY PATRICIA SMITH

for my family

CONTENTS

SERIES EDITOR'S PREFACE

The world has long flirted with implosion, and implosion has finally taken notice.

As I write this, we flail in a stubborn, insistent—and increasingly deadly—tangle of cultural, political, and global devastation. We once again speak of war as a given, a necessary and common occurrence. We're pummeled with unfiltered images of everything hatred can do, its snarl and grimace and spewed invectives, its stone in the pit of the belly. The air we breathe is no longer willing to nurture us, the earth no longer willing to be our unquestioning home. It's becoming increasingly difficult to find a direction that harbors solace or shelter.

And in the midst of our emotional desolation, we've been told—once again, dammit—that poetry is dead. It seems to die biannually, right on some crackpot schedule, its death often coinciding with the death of flared jeans, boy bands, and diet soda.

And once again—fresh from a deep dive into poetry that jolts, rearranges, rollicks, rebirths, convinces, destructs, and rebuilds—I am moved to dissent.

Poetry, at least the way it reaches me, has never been remotely close to quietus. It may occasionally be cloaked in a pensive or embarrassed silence or tangled in an overwrought and overwhelming barrage of language. It may be overly obsessed with sparing the delicate feelings of *someone* or maintaining the tenuous status of *something*. It can be tiring or inappropriate, or flat and studious, or heartless, or saddled with too *much* heart. Its pulse is sometimes so faint that its bare-there is often mistaken for that long-predicted demise.

At the biannual funeral, there is misguided celebration by tweed-swaddled critics, wheezing academics, and those who've spent their lives perplexed by poetry's omnipresent sway. It's a limit affair that makes them all feel better. But there's no weep or caterwaul, because actual poets—and gleeful lovers of sonnet, caesura, and stanza—have no reason whatsoever to grieve.

In fact, I come to you with reasons for rejoice, reasons to believe that poetry is not only alive, but that it is electric and naughtily raucous.

I must thank my tenacious and thoughtful readers, who consistently pass along the work that surprises, intrigues, and changes me. My readers are poets I revere—they are like me and unlike me, and the one thing they have in common is the consistency of their work. I've been contacted by people who say that the standard I've set for selection is virtually impossible.

I'm about to introduce you to four poets who seem, somehow, to have done the impossible.

Of course, picking a "winner" makes absolutely no sense in this context. Depending on the day and time I sat down to consider the finalists, their positions changed. The competition was just that heated. I want all of them to know, right now, that *any of you could have won.*

And all of them deserved to win.

Let's look at our—for lack of a better term—"runner-ups."

Adele Elise Williams's *Wager* was undoubtedly crafted to upend the familiar—both narratively and sonically—and turn it into something unflinchingly fresh. Language, as some of us know, exists to be fiddled with, and Williams, a storyteller who steadfastly refuses lyrical compliance, has a grand ol' time reintroducing us to what we assume we already know. I love a poet who runs rampant, rebelling against restraint—however, that by no means indicates a lack of discipline or a desire to cloak the work in "device." These poems hit home because they pull us into the poet's rampaging narrative, because we are all creatures of story who crave POVs that rouse us and redefine what we see. As a former "performance poet" (whatever that means these days), I took particular joy in reading *Wager* aloud—more than once, more than twice—and reveling in what Williams's deftly crafted ditties do to the air.

I mean, this is the opening of "Gal," the *first poem in the book*:

She's so helpless and the undertone
is spooky-ooky! She's so natural
and the assumption is heaven high
is gilded and gyrific, is like chakras.
I mean, placement for purpose. I mean,
outward burst. She's so blond!

And if that aural deliciousness puts you in the mood for play—not so fast. These poems swirl with shadow when you least expect it. The next time poetry dies, I highly suggest a massive infusion of—this.

Self-Mythology, by Chinese-Iranian poet Saba Keramati, is the book we need right now, as so many of us explore our hyphenated selves, searching for meaning in being not all one and not all the other, wondering if and where we are truly rooted.

But even as we turn inward for clues, we're a suspicious, judgmental lot, and so much of the volatile confusion that marks our days springs from a brash selfishness—our unwillingness to consider the person next to us, to learn what that person feels and believes, the tenets they live by. Keramati first confronts the formidable task of knowing the body and mind she inhabits—her backdrops and looming future, her vulnerabilities and failures, her reactions to loss and love, the experience of being two in the body of one. In her poem "The Act," she writes, "I'll always be / here, chameleoning myself // with every shift of the light."

So many writers are telling these stories—or making their best attempts to. Keramati avoids the many pitfalls of addressing a complex identity—you won't find confounding DIY tanglings of language or an unwavering eye fixed on the myriad metaphors of culture clash. *Self-Mythology*'s poems unreel with revelation, undaunted soul-searching, and crisp, deliberate lyric:

> Let me write myself here, with these symbols
> I claim to know, swear are in my lineage—
>
> proving myself to my own desire
> to be seen.

To be seen. To be heard. To grieve and rejoice and question out loud. All while so many demand a Black silence.

It has been decided, obviously by those who decide such things, that Black folks have made entirely too much noise about inconsequential things like— well, history. Our collective history, and the history of each one of us, the past that won't stop quivering in our chests. All those histories hastily being rescripted. Refocused. Disappeared.

In the midst of a country's fervent undertaking to render the Black voice inconsequential to both that country's backdrop and its future, Jeremy Michael Clark's insistence upon light—troubled though it may be—is imperative and rebelliously wrought. The huge story rests within the smaller one. Clark chronicles the fevered intersections of love and fear, and whole restless worlds reside in each line. Truths are unrelenting here—plain truths that agitate as they enlighten. There's so much of our lives that we hastily bury, hoping all that restless mayhem stays settled beneath us.

Clark, however, will not allow our conjured calm. Although there's a tender, assured turn to his lyric, he remains steadfastly focused on what trouble does to the light. His search for father is heartrending. Consider "Those That Flew":

> Before the house I believe is my father's
> I stand, a rust-flecked fence

between me & the answer. A latch
I can't lift. Rain comes & I say,

Is this how it's supposed to be?
Soaked, unable to shield myself

from what puddles at my feet.
I don't carry his name the way

I have his silhouette. Thunder sends birds
scattering & I count the seconds

between each clap to gauge how fast
the storm will come, though clearly,

it's here. From my mother
I learned my name. I know

their song, but not what I should call
those birds that flew.

You may think you've wandered this narrative landscape before. But you haven't. Not in this way.

And finally, the winner of this year's Miller Williams Poetry Prize—Alison Thumel's *Architect*.

I can't describe this book. I fill up every time I try. There's very little language huge enough to illustrate the depth of the poet's grief, her stark and tender transforming of it, her clenched containment of it as it pulses and bellows, straining to escape its borders.

There are so, so many ways to speak loss, but I've never experienced such structured tenderness, the building and rebuilding of what crafted the hollow. Alongside poems about Frank Lloyd Wright's creations, those glorious and lasting bodies, Thumel searches relentlessly for a lasting body her brother John might inhabit.

She has written often of John's death, and anyone who's barely lived through that grim upheaval will instantly recognize that anguished search for anything other than its bone-numbing torment.

Thumel builds and builds and loses and loses. And begins to build again.

Here I mark the spot where desolation
ended and began. Yet why mark this spot

if marking only remakes a misshapen
memory of the wound? The mark is dotted
like a line to form a charred and ugly
scar I run my fingers over, this path
I trace. Ended and began. Ended—see
I can mark the bounds of it. Nothing past
this wall I build, each brick a stitch I slip,
a slit I suture. Nothing—like trying
to see into a dark room before I dip
my hand far into that place. No small thing—
no stone, no wood, no work made of absence—
could mark you back into a present tense.

There are no words for what these words do.
And that's what it means to love poetry.

PATRICIA SMITH

SELF-MYTHOLOGY

THERE IS NO OTHER WAY TO SAY THIS

Every morning the sparrows sing   Every day there is another funeral

I am a fraud

A mouth is always open: 口   The tongue declares itself: زبان

I have to write this poem in English

I do not speak my mother's language   I do not speak my father's language

I am not grateful for this country

Mama, I am begging: 帮我   Baba, I am begging: کمک

I move closer to a life without language

I push the skin below my jaw   I pluck my eyebrow strays

I hunger for something I've yet to taste

Chopsticks rip the duck flesh   The blistered tomato splatters

The language burns and sticks

The country burns and burns

I hate saying America

Hearing America

I do not sing America and I do not want to

妈妈, I know all you gave up for this   بابا, I know it scares you to hear this

There are too many truths here

4

These are some of them

Without you there is no us   Without you there is no us

I am sorry

I am ungrateful

I am out of metaphors

What do these tanks remind you of   Does this new life still ring of prison

Exiled and found your way back to more of the same

A haunting   A prediction

I don't know if there's a better place for us

What refuge is this

What trickery

Oh

A lineage of pain   A once-held future

Would I give my existence for it

你的生命   زندگی تو

Like a river takes back its rain

Like a droplet ripples home

Hollowed

When I was small, my mouth was too.
The orthodontist implanted an expander,
gave the key to my mother.
I knelt in front of her every night. She twisted

metal into metal, widening my jaw.
A prayer. A baby bird.
My own teeth outgrowing me,
I worried about the rest of my bones:

would my skeleton suddenly sprout
past the tips of my fingers? My marrow
spill out into the world?
When I worry, I chew

the insides of my cheeks, peel the skin
from the edges of my fingertips,
making less of me.
The orthodontist shaved some tissue from my mouth:

For days, nothing but the taste of blood.
In nightmares, I devoured myself.
No hips, no belly. When I could eat again,
my mother said, *Don't.*

The Dream

Apples hang in the garden like fate
bruised by lies. There is a heaven only the good
can reach. What sounds beyond possibility often is.
Darkness leaks. The contract of hard work is not
enough. Fathers walk through the garden, plucking
fruit for their children. Their children are
greedy, even if they do not know it.
How can they not be, with all that was promised?
I open my mouth. Instead of a scream, a hundred
jasmine petals take wing. My father floats on them to a
kingdom where he is king. There are no subjects, only fruit.
Lemons he can send to me when I am sick. Plums for digestion.
My mother ripples into view, birthing me. I feel her
neck crane to look at me before I am
out. I feel her heart sink when I am
pronounced a girl. Feel the suffering, however
quiet, that is to come. I am born again and again,
reincarnated to the same self, the same fate.
Snow is falling. The cycle of water means it will fall again.
Tomorrow, perhaps. When I wake up,
urging myself to remember this: my father a king, my mother anew.
Visiting the possibilities of their lives,
wondering who they might be. I hear a whisper:
Xiǎo xīn. Have a small heart. There is too much to lose otherwise.
Yearning is dangerous. A small breeze turns into a great
zephyr: A door opens. Night pours out.

The Act

My fun fact is often that I exist. It's enough,
isn't it? A half-breed, a combo
you've never seen before.

Marvel at me and my three tongues.
Try to guess: which is the Chinese leg

and which is the Iranian. Hint:
one is hairier than the other. Oh—
I shaved them both.

Sometimes I wonder, if I slice up my parts,
could they fit into categories on the Census?

My features sectioned off, one by one.
A small tangerine, ripped open.
A smaller tear in its inside skin, the juice

slowly pooling in the gash,
slowly leaking.

But oh, look behind—
and you will see two knotted buns behind my ears!
Who am I being today? What will be the basis

of your hypothesis: the downward turn of my nose?
Or perhaps the small forehead. Look closer,

look closer. I do not mind at all.
You'll always be wrong, and I'll always be
here, chameleoning myself

with every shift of the light:
the underside of an oyster shell.

Are There Words for This

Baba buys me a pair of shoes, asks, *Does it feet?*
I ask Mama for pancakes,

she fills them with green onions.
I hear their accents only when they speak

to Americans. We give fake names
to the Starbucks barista. I learn

that which is too difficult to explain to white folk
is not worth my time.

I fill out government forms for my parents,
translate at the DMV. Legal jargon

the fourth language I speak.
I interpret between both sets of grandparents

before I hear the ABC's. I am the great genius
of my family lines, decoder of dialects,

articulation of my ancestors.
They take me to Disneyland to thank me

for being a good daughter and I have to ask for directions
from strangers. At a food stand, I buy a Mickey Mouse

lollipop. Shove his stupid upbeat voice
into my own mouth until it turns black.

Self-Portrait as Two

A twin. Exposed heart stretching outward. Two things can be true at once. Scissors and blood. In the mirror: a body. Cut the stray hairs around brows and lips. Hold the blade against the left thigh. Press against existing stretch marks. Skin trickles red: alive, but less. Cut the right thigh, too. One eye smaller than the other. Hand pressed against glass hand.

The symmetry of these halves never adds up. Fractions get fractioned the farther I move from myself. Imagine: a daughter, half of me already. Then—one half of each half. Then—barely me at all. What's the math I need to make that count? Imagine: a future woman. She is quarters or eighths. Will she be beautiful? Or will she look like me—at herself, in the mirror. The black of her eyes like a one-winged crow.

Chimera

One morning on the radio I hear a woman's voice singing: *Woman is a changeling, always shifting shape.* I am left to ponder a limitude of allowed selves. I was born two things at once, thought that made me rare. In turn, thought that made me important in some way. But here it is, clear over the airwaves: my own thoughts in someone else's mouth. So what's left? I admit I am interested in my own thinking, obsessed with discovery and answers because: how devastating to be wrong about who you are. Did god give us all the same questions? The way I break a promise is to forget myself. How monstrous to be always so confused. How animal. Oh, there is more of me on the inside. Oh, it is eating me alive.

⚚

                        a woman   *is a*

               shape.   a limitude of

                  thought   .

                                      what's left?

I am   obsessed with

                                          myself. How

monstrous   . How

          alive.

Inside Persepolis

It's called a site of ruins.
My father says it was an empire. I see nothing
but crumbled columns. A child drops
her mother's hand, reaches toward a stone

flower. A bird with two faces.
The lions trapped in a museum, far away.
A dragonfly lands in the dry earth.
Glimmering wings, like veins in a pale wrist.

The sun makes it hard to see. To think
there was once a river that flowed here.
A man spits on the ground: mud.
My mother in a headscarf,

her China skin so unlike my own.
The dust like a carpet over the bones.

Self-Portrait with Crescent Moon and Plum Blossoms

In the light of the moon that I only half-
belong to, my skin swells, stinging
and red as lanterns. This waning moon, its insides
full of goddesses and heartbreak, lore

I've learned from history books
and not my own blood. So take it,
China, take my blood. With these mosquitos
running rampant.   Suck the unbelonging

out of me. How long will it take to work?
I shape myself with the emblems I can gather.
Let me write myself here, with these symbols
I claim to know, swear are in my lineage—

proving myself to my own desire
to be seen.

Questions for the Outward Curve of My Stomach, Where I Sometimes Rest My Hand and Pretend to Be Pregnant

What have I inherited?

Is it salt?

Why does it sit so heavy in my stomach?

Aunties: why are our words for stomach and soul the same?

I am a woman: I was born with all my future children inside of me.

Is there a DNA test for this?

For salt?

Where does it all go, if I don't have a daughter?

Will it be the salt people sprinkle on their plums?

A lavender scrub to massage a woman's legs?

Returned to the earth, to feed a small cucumber garden?

Whose turn will it be to hold these glassy splinters?

Who can I assure the hurt will pass?

Whose hand to hold?

Whose belly to clutch when the jagged edges cut deep inside?

My aunties once scrubbed a chair for two hours after I bled on it.

What's Lost

I have always shrouded myself in poems.
I thought I was clever but I was hiding.

There is so much left to understand.
There are things I do not know about my ancestry

because I am afraid to ask.
Where would I put it down?

I want to unearth what was buried,
hold it in my hands and pick it apart,

shake its dust loose and read
the scatterings like a fortune.

Instead I write and I guess, translate
the fragments into something meaningful.

I do not know if that saves us
any pain.

I once saw a poet I loved at the gym:
silver hair stringy and wet. Drenched and tired.

I think she made eye contact with me.
I think she knew I recognized her.

I think she could tell I have read *The Glass Essay*
a hundred times over

and over again. I think she could tell.
I think she looked away on purpose.

What she didn't remember: I met her once,
backstage at a performance of an ancient play

she translated. When did Antigone get so old?
(I know Greek history about as well as my own.)

I lost my languages and so I wanted an explanation:
Where does unbelief begin?

Where is god? The Chorus?
Will you leave me so voiceless and misunderstood?

I turned to ask her, but she was gone.
Just a trail of wet footprints.

The Birth of Language

Light was his first spoken creation.
And who gave him speech?

Those who peddle god
make him sound benevolent.

Let there be poetry, he said.
Language can twist like a snake.

God made, and so he birthed,
and so he was a mother.

He can make anything sound beautiful.

Cento for Loneliness & Writer's Block & the Fear of Never Being Enough, Despite Being Surrounded by Asian American Poets

There is a house in me. It is empty. I empty it.
When the sadness comes
in a shroud,
there's the perpetual feeling of being.

A thirst for the self.
When I'm melancholy like this, it's so nice
to wake up and come back to me.
Loneliness is still time spent—

I, I've come to know, is the essence.
I wash my hands in ink.
I haven't been able to finish
building a house.

I wrote the word *snow*.
I hurry home as though someone is there waiting for me.

Haibun for Learning 中文 on Duolingo

My mother tells me that when she loses her memory, she will stop speaking English. She asks how I will be able to speak to her then, and I respond, *You won't lose your memory*. This is not an answer. It is its own kind of loss. My grandmother has lost her hearing, and also her hearing aids. She yells into the phone when she calls. She calls my mother because she does not have my phone number. Because there is not much she can say to me. *Hello. Are you well. Have you eaten sweet noodles today.*

I am trying my best and every morning at ten I receive an alert that my best is not fast enough. By then, the coffee has gone cold, I have completed my morning exercises, and still I do not speak a language I have a name in.

Owl flight is silent;
the feathers break turbulence
into quietude.

With a dull blade, I cut the lamb's tongue

I pretend it was never alive. I am a hypocrite, not a vegetarian. The tongue is tougher than I expect, and I roll mine inwards. I am not strong, and the cutting takes two minutes. The last bit of muscle rips like a ghost from a body. My aunties clap for me. They say good girl, they say mashallah. My mouth is cold and full of spit.

In the Smoke of the Wild Rue Seeds

It rises like a djinn, crackles and burns
as it shapes itself into a forked tongue,
the ends coming to snatch my eyes.
This is not what the Internet said
would happen. Esphand purifies, protects.
Or so the superstition goes. The tears
sting like vinegar, and the smoke shifts
into a chorus of open mouths
laughing at my ignorance. There is no respite:
this is the air I have made. I've burned
what was meant to be planted.
My malevolence surprises me, as if shattering
a mirror and gazing upon fractals
of blurred history, unrecognizable and still
familiar in the brokenness.
The smoke's sharp edge scratches my throat,
searching for a way out. I know its desperation.
Does it matter where a thing is learned,
if I am trying my best? I do not know
who else in my family burns, or burned.
Does this rite still cleanse if I don't believe in it all the way?
With a swallow, I calm what's left of the flame,
open a window of this empty house.
The half of me whose ritual this is
was never supposed to be here.

Self-Portrait Alone in the Kitchen

My body seems to grow in unwelcome places.
I wait for the kettle to boil.

I sit on a stool, hunched over, curled
like I am rotting. I train myself to shrink.

I train myself to starve. I grow soft
instead of smaller. A body

with a mind of its own. I drink tea
so I can taste something. A trick.

A drop of honey on the tongue
gilds my insides. The kettle whistles high

and angry. I wish for the water to melt me.
Maybe then I'll glisten. The folds in my belly

rivers of gold instead. Reflecting.
My mother once showed me 饿:

the character for hunger. A self
being eaten. When my stomach growls,

I imagine it is eating itself, it is eating me,
it will make me thin like my mother.

Invocation

God is so singular in his existence.
It must be lonely. All that power.
No one to share it with. I think it is a price
I would pay, lonely as I am.
I have been looking for another like me
and I have yet to find them. Still
I am not so bold to think I am beyond
imagination. But would god exist without
our thoughts of him? To think what has been done
in his name is all holy—No. There is violence
beyond what I can think of, and still it happened.
All this to say, my conception of myself
is solitary without worship. What's the difference
between a person and a prayer?
If unfulfilled, then godforsaken.
I dream of a future me, and maybe she
is the god I invoke, the one I beseech to live.

Those Who Live

for Vincent Chin

I've come to where he is buried,
looking for answers. I am ashamed
of what I did not know. Once,

I made it to the front gate of the cemetery.
A funeral procession of Fords
with American flags stopped me.

A baseball bat flashed through my mind.
It's the anniversary of his death again.
Today is the first time

I've made it this far. Usually, I stop
driving at the red post marking what's left
of Detroit Chinatown. Or, should I say,

the red post that is all
that's left of Detroit Chinatown.
The years pass so quickly. I've lived

a short distance away for so many of them now.
His ghost always with me but unnamed
for so long. I had to google the mural in memoriam,

across from the new dog hotel and tattoo parlor.
There's a phrase I've heard for years now:
steel, not chopsticks. The suggestion being

one is stronger than the other. But did you know
he was an orphan?
I call my mother and ask

if she's ever heard his name. She says no.
I keep looking. The headstones grow
blurry before my eyes. Strange,

how the graves of the murdered are so hard to find.

Dream of Liminal Space

Sorrow perfumes the air. It is night, inside and out. The moon leaks red across the sky. It has cracked. Its fracture: a doorway. There is no way to know what's within. Be it secrets, or hyacinth, or a room so filled with lit candles there is nowhere to step without danger. Only a crossing is possible. Only a change is waiting.

Nocturne in Which I Give Myself unto Another

I fear fire because the moon gave me none.
But to him I give myself willingly:
the moon rose with fire at his birth.
What burned now balms. Salvation
from the self is all I have ever asked for.
I love him because I have never known another
man so scared to be wrong. Belief in omniscience
is easier than questioning: Do we believe in god
because we want to believe in a good man?
He admits he does not know. I revere that.
An open window. A future.

The God Who Ate His Children

Is it possible that I understand, from some innate emptiness,
how it feels to want to put something back inside myself,
the fear of what I've created overpowering the love I have for it—
for me—so much so that I cry when I think about Saturn?

At night, the stars float on a black lake, rippling in harmony
with the wilderness and the turn of the planets
in a way so human it strikes me with such envy that I want to cry
out to them (as if they can hear, as if they are anything but fire): oh,
the teeth, the bones, the skin, the hunger.

Devotion

Some nights, I let my lover between my thighs.
Tonguing a secret place.
Some nights, I strive to out-please him.
His flesh in my mouth. My hair in his palm.

On my knees: an offering.
I feel nothing, but holy—desire sacrificed.
The pleasure on my lover's face: a prayer.
I have divined his faith.

I touch my own longing, my lust unholy.
This greed makes me powerful.
Should I command he worship me?
A god can do such a thing.

My gasp, my taking: acceptance.
My acceptance: a resurrection.

Fire Season Grows Longer

What's left of one fire can start another.
A small gust of wind, and this dry earth alights

like a vengeance, unafraid and unstoppable.
Then, new growth. Who is worthy of it?

The sun shining where it could not reach before.
This is a threat, even in its beauty.

It feels too simple to say I was not made
for this. Who was? I am less important than I think

myself, make less of a difference than I desire.
I fear the warning signs with each revolution

around the sun. When I say this is not a home,
do I mean the Earth or America? Neither

is the center of the universe. I have never lived
anywhere else. It is all I know: the scorch of it,

the fresh dirt, the possibilities. Its dissonance
and violence; beautiful, burning violence.

Disappointing Things

Snow that turns to dirty slush after being walked over. An orange with a seed in the very last bite. A colorful rug with an indiscernible pattern. Friends who tell lies. The bottom of a grown-up's foot, when compared to a baby's. An itching scab, unscratchable, because it is not quite skin.

My father tells me not to insult god with my rituals. I bite into a plum; the pit scrapes against my teeth. I taste pink lemonade in a dream so distinctly the summer grass tickles the roof of my mouth. Awake, there is only water.

World War 3 Is Trending on Twitter

"America, ignore the window and look at your lap"
—Solmaz Sharif

With every news outbreak, I think to write
about war, but I don't know
enough. *Freedom* as a word disgusts me,
its underbelly danger, colonialism, dirty
secrets hidden from the citizens it's sworn to protect.
Citizen, too, a word that can be taken away.
The words, the safety, the deep shameful thought
buried in the back of my mind:
I am an American. Though I have never liked that about myself—
it is true. The word *America*
a shield I never wanted to carry.
Yes, my parents lived through wars and revolutions;
the key word is *lived*.
Sought refuge so I could learn to write
in English. The word *war* is one of soft sounds
in the mouths of those who have never heard bombs.

At the lakeshore I am reminded that we are different

In the sand, we take off our shoes.
My lover says this is his favorite place in the world.

This is not an ocean. It looks like one.
There is no place I love enough to call it mine.

At this horizon, I forget what I am looking at.
I am here, wondering which water is a grave and which is just a beach.

What pastoral is this: me, against this whiteness?
Around us, does anyone know where we are?

I am here, and I am in his parents' living room
being introduced to a new girlfriend, a new baby, his family ever-expanding

and they are all white, white, white.
He tells me to look at the sunset and not around us.

I think it's because he's starting to understand. Around us,
a white woman talks loudly on her phone, drowning out the call of the gulls.

Another in flip-flops flings sand behind her with every step.
Refuses to go barefoot, complains about the burning on the bottoms of her
    delicate feet.

Take me home, I want to say, but I do not know where I mean.
I've walked three miles in dunes now and I am in the same country.

My feet bending in unnatural ways.
Everyone is sweating.

If I close my eyes, I could pretend it's just us.
We are just two people in love; there is nothing complicated about it.

Once, his parents called mine brave
instead of forced to be here.

Ars Poetica Ghazal

Open the way a door opens:
away from me. Like the mouth of a river opening,

softly against the rocks, its own babble enough.
The way a swallow chirps, so open

and sharp against the sky. The way I yawn
when I think of a yawn, instinctive and thus open.

Before I speak I must admit poetry
will not change the world. I entreat an opening

without force. In the face of such suffering,
I name: I can only own my open

mouth and the deed to my own thinking.
I think myself alive and so I am. So I open

against authority, to think I matter. O,
with three names in my mouth, I open.

Cento for Loneliness & Writer's Block & the Fear of Never Being Enough, Despite Being Surrounded by Asian American Poets II

This sadness I feel tonight is not my sadness.
When my heart returns in the solitude,
it can think itself and think itself into existence.
A lyric summoning.

Oh, how I love the resoluteness—
How to love like water loves,
in the way that stars keep their distance.
O loneliness, my body responds.

Our forms, our least known selves—
I just wanted to write again and say:
Don't think, when you melt in sorrow,
that without warm blood a creature cannot dream.

I never told anyone this story:
I told myself I lost nothing.

My Aquarius moon won't let me rest

It says, *Remember when you lost a tampon inside yourself?* It says, *Scratch your head. Open your eyes.* It sends memories I'd forgotten. I'm forced to wonder what forgetting means, if I can be reminded so easily. My moon puts me back in my body when I dream about levitating. When I was younger I dreamt I could fly so often I began to think it was true. Maybe it happened. Maybe it was a dream. Maybe it happened once and I remembered it in a dream. What else has gone wandering deep in this body, what else has slipped from memory? I like to think it's only the bad, and when I put my fingers inside myself my moon dips through my window and says, *Come with me.*

Ode to Birthmark

Before my mother had me, she miscarried
        for the first time. I am blessed by her losing,
as all children are. On my right calf:

its mark. Large and blemished,
        a permanent memory of my parents'
first daughter. Elder version of myself,

whose skin, a little deeper than mine,
        stayed in our mother's womb
longer than her body. From poetry,

I learned to dive into the wreck.
        From this flecked skin, to hold on
to what I cannot prove

but still know to be true. To hold
        it with the tightness of my palm
against a hot cup of tea, which is to say,

until it fevers red with welcomed ache.
        The ache and not the story of the ache,
I remind, though I can't help but assign

narrative to the stain of myself.
        There's a reason for my imperfection:
time and skin stitched together.

I have been mythologizing myself
        since I observed my own other,
this stamp of loss, this dapple

of scar as if gazed upon by light
        through the dense lace between birch leaves.
What shone inside my mother?

Relics for My Future

mother's strand of pearls

father's briefcase of handwritten stories

these poems

holding on to temporary

an unyielding grip

asylum (protection or institution?)

visa with an end-date

marriage with an end-date

the permanence of emergency

the capitalist myth

the body politic

scraps of survival

an attic for artifacts

a daughter for memories

Rewrite: I Go Back

For a moment, it's all still there. A mirage
of the California heat. Wavering between now

and memory. I can see them in the past, at this window.
The gleam of the blue neon "open" sign above
their heads like a flood ready to wash them away.

He is younger than I've ever seen him,
drinking chocolate milk. Is this the first time,

or the third? I know he came here more than once.
Not for the grocery store chocolate milk—
for the woman behind the cash register. She is bright-eyed,

yet perhaps it was this day he saw the faint rubble
of Tiananmen Square left on her cheeks.

Should I go in and tell her it will never
wash away? Or maybe this is the moment
she learns that, too. The man drinking chocolate milk

still smells of Iranian dirt and bomb-smoke.
In a year, they'll be married. She'll be pregnant.

Should I go in and tell them that now is the best time
to buy a house? Right now, they are fading,
but they still believe in so much.

They don't need to know their apartment
will be too small, that their one child will be

their last, or that their love has an expiration date.
They will fight and there will be anger
they can't forget. They will suffocate

in their small apartment, their daughter will cry
alone in her bed while their screams rattle

the kitchen glassware. Their insults will hang
on the doorframes. I could go in and tell them.
But what if these sweet moments are enough

for a lifetime? What could they do differently,
anyhow? Maybe we can remember

past the hurt. The more I remember something,
the more it seems to shift. I remember
someone spat on me, once, and I said nothing.

Should I go in and tell them?

Accidental Loss

It looks like you're miscarrying,
the doctor says (twice), speculum
cranking wider, the walls of my vagina
tightening to protect me and (possible?)
(dying?) baby (?). The doctor is scraping
something from inside me, the sound
of my naked exposition echoing
as I clench. *Relax*, the doctor says,
but I do not hear. The squish
of discharge rising loud to meet my ears.

       I keep air in my mouth like it is a secret.
       I think I would be a good mother—I would not force
       her to play piano. I once told a stranger my mother
       was pregnant. I know not to do that again.
       I learn from my mistakes. I prepare for worst-case
       scenarios. This is one I never considered: impossible
       futurity. I am bleeding with my legs in stirrups.
       When I shift in discomfort, I rip
       the paper beneath my sweating back.

You weren't trying to get pregnant,
right? (Does it matter?) I call my lover
and he is relieved? concerned? My vagina aches.
I call my insurance company and they do not answer.
I leave a message: am I covered?
My nipple itches from the crinkle
of the white plastic gown I was wearing
just moments ago (a different person then).
I drive myself home. I do not remember
crossing the bridge.

Ghosts

roam through
the streets of China,

the air humid
with spirits rustling

around. They are hungry
for something only the dead

can taste. Such as wind,
such as whispers,

such as the stillness after an echo.
I am here to speak

to my great-grandmother,
but I cannot call to her

because she had no name.
Instead I hum a lullaby

under my breath,
longing for some sort

of phantom reckoning.
It is a song

I do not know,
sung in a graveyard

of the living.
The bodies are echoing

with words
I only slightly recognize:

Bù. Don't wander
too far, the ghosts tell me.

I have tried.
Give me the answers

I do not know
the questions to.

A chrysanthemum blooms in boiling water. It does not drown.

I am begging to be haunted.

The Return

I ask my father if I am covering my hair for god
or for men, and he says, *Government*,
which feels like he is saying both.

The plane moves between thresholds—
Gazed upon and compelled. Ruled and regulated.
For months now I have bled, lost an egg,

and I must confess I still do not feel grown.
I try to render each strand of myself invisible.
In the airport, my aunties giggle at my caution.

No one around seems frightened by the guards.
Men here are the same as everywhere. The stakes, too.
That night I dream I am a child again, and genderless,

or at least innocent. Or maybe they are the same thing.
My father holds me in the sea and I laugh
as each wave laps against my back. The nape

of my neck is bare. My mother stands on the sand.
Her long black overcoat seems to grow behind her,
snaking against the horizon.

Cento for Loneliness & Writer's Block & the Fear of Never Being Enough, Despite Being Surrounded by Asian American Poets III

Today, when faced with such a spectacle,
I stand quietly and allow this quality to permeate air around me.
All I wanted was snow.
I hold things I cannot say in my mouth—

I'm a poem someone else wrote for me.
How can I say this more clearly? It was like opening a heavy book:
snow melts into a pool of clear water.
It could be colder just now but it isn't.

In small American cities
I dream of suffering together with my people.
There is mythology planted in my mouth which is like sin.
I cannot help but know the words.

Hide me in a room:
I will never be the same.

In the Beginning There Were Fires

When I was a child, I touched a red-hot stove. My mother washed my hand under cool water, kissed my burnt flesh. The skin grew back without a scar.

The pain: a memory.

Every year, more of California burns. I hear my mother's voice in the fresh earth, asking me to come back home. I flinch from the question. It has burned a blackened heart. If I could reach back under my skin, I know I could touch it, and with my fingertip

make it crumble.

Self-Portrait without Plans or Prayers

In the mornings I uncouple the curtains,
let the natural sunlight in, save

some money on the electricity bill. When I retreat
to the living room, where the piano remains

untouched and dusty, I lose track
of myself. Time feels unnecessary.

The next time I pay attention,
it is dark. I let the curtains kiss again.

The light from inside the house reveals too much,
exposes me in sweaty polka-dot pajamas

to happy neighbors who might be passing by.
The fears I keep hidden: be seen? Or be

seer? What future? Nothing has changed
for a long time. When I turn my head: a shadow,

the faint dancing of tree branches,
a crack in this curtained universe.

I watch the wind on the wall.
The light quivering of the outside world.

Every moment becomes more chilling,
the night seeping its way through my home's

cheap insulation. I am not keeping track,
but time makes its way into my brain,

and everything with it: passing.

What Remains

Sitting on a plane, just three years old, I asked my mother, *Are we in heaven?* I asked my mother and she said no. *No, I don't believe in heaven.* My mother did not believe in heaven and so I did not believe in heaven. I did not believe in heaven so when I prayed it wasn't to god. It wasn't to god, it was to the earth. To the earth, I prayed: *Please make my mother stop crying.* My mother cried for so long. She cried for so long that there were no more tears. There were no more tears and so it was no longer crying. She was empty. She told me she felt empty. I picked her a rose. The rose came from our garden but I put it in her bed. In my mother's bed I held her hand. I held her hand and prayed once more: *Please make my mother happy again.* With our palms touching, the pink of my mother's cheeks returned. I remember watching clouds wisp behind us, disappearing the way I disappear into my mother's long black hair when she bends down to kiss my forehead. I am a part of her again. She is full with me. Sitting on a plane in my mother's lap, I asked, *Where else could we be?*

After 9/11 We Wonder If We Should Ever Celebrate

Remember: we have done this
before. We have stood with our fathers,
watched the east. Yes, the sky

looks different tonight,
and maybe it is. After all,
we are still here:

still laughing, still jumping.
Consider: each spark a small firework,
each leap a small delight.

Listen: once, I was afraid to jump
but my mother did not know.
Our hands clasped; my knees buckled

while my arm went with hers. My elbow
popped out of its house, still creaks
like a rusty door hinge when I try to use it.

Wednesdays are for truths.
Sayeh: shadow.
Sadeh: simple.

Danger lurks in the eye of the fire.
We have been jumping over it
since we were children.

We have landed on the other side
of the flame, our feet soft
in the sand.

Self-Portrait with Womanhood

I remove the hair from my legs in the shower,
debate how much time to spend on the rest
of me. The bath is already emptying slowly.
I have inherited thick black hair.
A cheap pink razor will never remove it completely.
It was not until I was loved that I became
unembarrassed of my body. The razor glides
up my inner thigh, and I remember pinching
the fat of it, wishing the skin closer to the bone.
I confess I want a daughter but my stomach
already hangs too far out, folds
in on itself when I bend. I do not pretend
it doesn't, nor do I shave the thin
trail of hair that lines it.
But still I wish it different.
My hair wraps around itself at the bottom
of the tub. How can I raise a daughter
without shame? Which scars will she notice?
My mother's: a polio vaccine.
Mine: self-inflicted.
My beloved has touched them, kissed them,
traced their ridges. To be loved by a man
feels ordinary. To be healed by him,
unsettling. I am no emblem
for how to exist. I drag the razor
down the mound of myself:
I feel like a girl again. The water rises.
I am still my own daughter.

Lump

The doctor tells me I am too young for a mammogram. I do not tell her about the three new white hairs I found yesterday. The fish in the waiting room do not understand the concept of the ocean, do not fathom that there is larger water for them. Some fish only grow to the size of their captive homes. Such cruelty. All those years wishing myself smaller, of course my body would enact its own revenge. A poet once told me to write like I know I am going to die. I wait for the biopsy results, thumbing the scarred skin at my breast. Benign. A warning, then. To find a new wish. To move beyond myself.

Eye

egotistical only child / lone plane in a cloudless sky / caged dog / unfinished map of a woman / blurred story / mocking 5:17 pm / calloused ghost / honeyed poem / song of / of / stubborn attention / concentric histories / stretched light / gazing futureward / inward / unearned metaphor / oh utterance / oh confession of so much breath / oh song / oh self

Self-Mythology

I learn and I mourn
for not learning earlier.

The mint grew but was not eaten.
A harvest turned to waste.

The old brick of this house keeps
the wandering night air cold and inside.

I cannot fathom my mother
before she was my mother.

What forgiveness is necessary,
for someone doing their best?

There is no relief, only the swell
of an inward tide back toward the self.

I learn and I mourn.
There is no anger,

only truth. Only consequence.
Only: I, gazing at the past

of my own body, the shell
of myself melting, meaning I will drip

to a future where I am a mother;
am my mother, and all is what she helped create.

One day, too, my daughter will break
upon the shore, and still

she will float back.
I see it endlessly.

Inside the Museum, a Remnant

Between us there is glass.

      A simple bowl: blue and white.

My shadow-self mirrored: a shape without features.

      Chrysanthemums around the edge.

The materials Iranian. The pattern Chinese.

      Did I exist before this moment?

In the glass I am the bowl.

      A simple bowl: blue and white.

This—a part of my own history I did not know.

      In museums I do not always read the fine print.

A simple bowl: blue and white.

      Today, it is imperative to pay attention.

At some point in time, my father's country met my mother's.

      Traded with each other.

A simple bowl: blue and white.

      Delicately crafted that which centuries later would find me.

I am not well-versed in history.

I cannot tell you why this bowl exists.

To eat is too simple an answer.

A simple bowl—

To wait, buried, until my eyes rested upon it?

We call impossible things miracles.

For the first time, I feel less impossible.

Miraculous, instead, is so much of what came before.

Caught in the back of my throat is an ancient scream.

I admire my own stolenness. There is nothing else.

This bowl, and me: one taken, one aching to be found.

What will we do with what is left of us?

Let future historians find me buried in the same place as my ancestors.

A country that doesn't exist. Never existed.

For now: go home, make chrysanthemum tea.

Tattoo a garland of chrysanthemums around my thigh.

My whole life I have been looking to corroborate my own existence.

How many years have I been existing,   unaware of my self?

A simple bowl: blue and white.

America in Spring

My lover has overturned the earth
in our backyard to grow roses

for me. I want their water, want to boil
their petals in a copper pot

like my mother used to do. She learned it
from my father's mother, and so it falls to me.

It is tedious work but she would say sweet tastes sweeter
after bitterness. When I drop a fistful of dirt

some clings beneath my fingernails.
My lover runs the hose for me.

Is this the dirt we mean when we say America?
The dirt of it so easily washed away?

I do not want to believe in the possibility of America
that politicians cite, and yet—

America, you are responsible for me and I do not mean
simply that I was safeguarded to you.

My parents crossed bitter oceans for you,
so without you I have nothing to return to.

You could cut me in half. Send the left side with my mother,
right with my father. Shape what's missing out of clay

from their lands and still I would not belong.
America, do you see my dilemma?

I have this body, these words, some dirt,
and the future I see within you. The sweet.

I want to grow more roses.
I want to make more of myself.

What altar do I create for my daughter?
What questions will she have about you?

Here I stand, contradicting myself.
America, is that your magic?

Reflections of Heaven

The call of a nighthawk rings out into the night.
Between sky and water, only blue surrounds.
This lake, a reflection of heaven. In Chinese,
heaven is just a house in the sky, and the sky is empty.

Between sky and water, only blue surrounds.
Morning glories, once open, turn inward on themselves.
Heaven is just a house in the sky. Is it empty?
It is turning black. The only blue the moon's halo.

Morning glories, once open, turn inward on themselves;
their heaven a self-creation, their house their own bodies.
They are turning black. The moon's blue halo
fading behind a cloud, like the door of a house closing.

I create a heaven, a house outside of my own body.
A home is so hard to find. I am disappearing,
fading behind a cloud, like the door of a house closing.
All that's left: a perfect moon.

A home is so hard to find. I am disappearing
beneath the waves, swelling to the shore.
In Farsi, when something is perfect, it is the moon.
How long can I search for a place that doesn't exist?

Waves always swell to the shore. Some things belong,
like the call of a nighthawk ringing out in the night.
How long can I search for a place that doesn't exist?
This lake, a reflection of heaven.

Self-Portrait as a Bowl of Persimmons

It is true: all words are invented. I have names in three languages. What's the word for this?

My mother brings home persimmons from the market. She names them. Washes them gently, so as not to bruise.

My father opens the persimmons. He names them. Reveals how they are somehow darker on the inside than the out.

I eat persimmons, ruminating on poetry. Turning the words of it over in my mouth with each chew. Each bite a new language. With the taste comes the remembering. So much *what are you*. There are two kinds of persimmons. In English, they are the same.

I define myself: a hybrid child, heart-shaped and ready. I celebrate the sweet flesh of myself. Call myself. Name myself. Create a fortune of myself. I am looking for words, but why?

The persimmons are right there.

Feast

The eye of the fish in the hot pan stares at me.
It changes color as it cooks. The savor fills our home.
I am hungry. I want to eat.

I remember watching my mother
buy fish from the market, the smell
overwhelming. I used to cover my nose as she guided
us through the crowd of shoppers, her sense of direction innate.

What I know to do is balance, never let
one flavor overtake the others. Everything is delicate.
I measure through my body: the peppercorn
the size of the first fold of my index finger, the fennel
the cupped palm of my hand. Cloves the length of my thumb.
Five stars of anise. A pinch of cinnamon.

In the autumn, trout come to the river to spawn
and then die. To die in the same place you're born
is a strange kind of blessing. The scales of the fish
so iridescent they catch the reflection of the water, turn
invisible. I remember watching my mother
light incense, watching the smoke dissipate.

When we eat the top half of the fish, we uncover
its bones, translucent in its flesh.
We lift its skeleton to make way for the rest of it;
the head and tail remain attached at each end.
You know I cannot bear to eat the head. You put it on your plate,
take a bite of its cheek. Tell me it's delicious.
Tell me I cooked it right.

NOTES

In "The Act," the sentence "I do not mind at all" is borrowed from the Zora Neale Hurston essay "How It Feels to Be Colored Me."

"Self-Portrait as Two" is written after the painting *The Two Fridas* by Frida Kahlo.

In "Chimera," the line "woman is a changeling, always shifting shape" is borrowed from the Florence and the Machine song "King," written by Florence Welch.

"What's Lost" is written after "The Glass Essay" by Anne Carson. The line "Where does unbelief begin?" is borrowed directly from the poem. The lines "I wanted an explanation" and "Where would I put it down?" are in reference to but not exact lines from the same poem.

"The Birth of Language" takes its title from the Lucille Clifton poem of the same name.

"Cento for Loneliness & Writer's Block & the Fear of Never Being Enough, Despite Being Surrounded by Asian American Poets" is made of lines borrowed from (in order of appearance): Diana Khoi Nguyen, Fatimah Asghar, Solmaz Sharif, Jaswinder Bolina, Victoria Chang, Sasha Stiles, Tarfia Faizullah, Ocean Vuong, Aria Aber, Cathy Linh Che, Chen Chen, Suji Kwock Kim, Brenda Shaughnessy, and Kazim Ali.

The title of "Those Who Live" is borrowed from a speech by the Reverend Jesse Jackson, who took time out of his presidential bid to show support for the Asian American community and the "Justice for Vincent Chin" campaign.

"Cento for Loneliness & Writer's Block & the Fear of Never Being Enough, Despite Being Surrounded by Asian American Poets II" is made of lines borrowed from (in order of appearance): Li-Young Lee, Yone Noguchi, Jenny Xie, Meena Alexander, Marilyn Chin, Ed Bok Lee, Sandra Lim, Eugene Gloria, Cathy Linh Che, Paisley Rekdal, Mahmoud Darwish (trans. Fady Joudah), Kimiko Hahn, Hannah Sanghee Park, and Garrett Hongo.

The poem referenced throughout "Ode to Birthmark" is Adrienne Rich's "Diving into the Wreck." The italicized line is borrowed directly from that poem.

"Rewrite: I Go Back" is in direct conversation, in both title and trajectory, with Sharon Olds's "I Go Back to May 1937."

"Cento for Loneliness & Writer's Block & the Fear of Never Being Enough, Despite Being Surrounded by Asian American Poets III" is made of lines borrowed from (in order of appearance): C. Dale Young, Mei-mei Berssenbrugge, Cathy Park Hong, Justin Chin, Sarah Gambito, Oliver de la Paz, Arthur Sze, Rick Barot, Adrienne Su, Ha Jin, Tina Chang, Sarah Kay, Aimee Nezhukumatathil, and Yanyi.

"After 9/11 We Wonder If We Should Ever Celebrate" references the چهارشنبه‌سوری holiday, a celebration before the spring new year, in which celebrants jump over bonfires in a cleansing ritual. The beginning of the poem references Walt Whitman's "On the Beach at Night."

"Inside the Museum, a Remnant" takes place at the Detroit Institute of Arts. The line "What will we do with what is left of us?" is borrowed from Mahmoud Darwish's poem "Who Am I, Without Exile?," translated by Fady Joudah.

"Eye," "America in Spring," and "Self-Portrait as a Bowl of Persimmons" all briefly reference Walt Whitman's "Song of Myself."

"Self-Portrait as a Bowl of Persimmons" is indebted to Li-Young Lee's poem "Persimmons."

ACKNOWLEDGMENTS

Thank you to the editors at the following journals and magazines in which poems from this book, sometimes in earlier versions and/or under different titles, first appeared: *Adroit Journal, AGNI, Anomaly, Barren Magazine, Flypaper Lit, Gulfstream Lit, Glass: A Journal of Poetry, Hayden's Ferry Review, Homology Lit, LitHub, Longleaf Review, Passages North, Poet Lore, Poetry Online, Santa Ana River Review, Radar Poetry, Seventh Wave, Tinderbox Poetry Journal, Vagabond City Lit*, and *Quarterly West*. Thank you, as well, to Alternating Current Press and Green Linden Press for republishing some poems in the anthologies *Best Small Fictions 2023* and *Essential Voices: Poetry of Iran and Its Diaspora*.

I am eternally grateful to Patricia Smith for seeing this book, believing in it, and selecting it for the Miller Williams Poetry Series. I am honored to be part of this legacy. Thank you, as well, to the entire team at the University of Arkansas Press for their work in making this book come to fruition.

I am in awe of the friends I've met through poetry, all of whom have helped with this book in one way or another: Sarah Ghazal Ali and Hajjar Baban, to whom I am forever grateful for their endless support and gentle pushing to believe in myself; Yasmine Ameli and Juliana Roth, who help me remember I am a person in addition to a writer; and Joyce Chen and Bretty Rawson, for giving me the opportunity to develop the opening poem of this collection, as well as the space and time to finish the book. Thank you to Gauri Awasthi, Ariana Benson, Jody Chan, Stephanie Choi, JJ Peña, Yasmine Roukiaya, and Tae Min Suh for being writers I can learn from, in addition to loving and supportive friends.

I'm lucky enough to have made wonderful friends at UC Davis, where this book was first conceived. Thank you to Jennifer Ahlquist, Mangai Arumugam, Meredith Herndon, my press mate Michael Mlekoday, and Kelly Thomas for reading my early drafts.

I am so grateful to the poetry community for allowing me to know so many wonderful people that I simply cannot name them all individually. I would not be the writer I am today without the feedback and encouragement of all the friends and workshop cohorts I met along this journey. You are all brilliant. You have all blessed me. Thank you for helping me and my book become what we are today.

I also want to thank the following teachers who have all bestowed lasting knowledge upon me: Lisa Makman and Cody Walker at the University of Michigan, Margaret Ronda and Katie Peterson at UC Davis, Leila Chatti, Eduardo C. Corral, Solmaz Sharif, and Yanyi. Good teachers are precious, and few and far between. Thank you all for your kindnesses, and your magic.

There are also many organizations to which I am indebted, without which my poetry would not have had nearly as many opportunities to grow: the UC Davis Humanities Institute, the *Kenyon Review* Writers Workshop, Writing x Writers, *Frontier Poetry*, Sundress Publications, Tin House Summer Workshop, *Split Lip Magazine*, *Sundog Lit*, OneWorld Ideas in Action Workshop, Community of Writers and its Lucille Clifton Memorial Scholarship, the Unterberg Poetry Center, and the Seventh Wave. Thank you to all the people I've met in these spaces.

Some of what has sustained me over the years of writing this book include: peonies, ducklings, Dearborn & the Bay, campfires, parallel play, group chats, homegrown pumpkins & their vining tendrils, oat milk, acts of revolution, collaging & ceramics, art museums, rooftops, tote bags, macarons, June Jordan, independent literary magazines, noodle soups, the lakes, blankets, nighttime laughter, candy gift boxes, figs & axles, bookstores, the sound of small bells, friendship, resistance, holding hands. And Biscuit & Bobby, sweet cats who have taught me new ways to love, new ways to see, new ways to measure time—and who deserve their own sentence.

To my extended families: thank you for supporting me from near and far, through languages close and distant.

To Nick, my beloved: thank you for making a home with me. I would follow you to the moon.

To my parents, who made it clear in no uncertain terms that their dreams for me were that I follow my own: I owe you my life, and every good thing that has ever happened to me. This book would be impossible without your love.